Measuring the Weather

W9-BHK-008

Temperature

Alan Rodgers and Angella Streluk

Heinemann Library
Chicago, Illinois

© 2003 Reed Educational & Professional Publishing
Published by Heinemann Library,
an imprint of Reed Educational & Professional Publishing,
Chicago, Illinois
Customer Service 888-454-2279
Visit our website at www.heinemannlibrary.com

Design by Storeybooks
Originated by Ambassador Litho Limited
Printed in Hong Kong/China

07 06 05 04 03
10 9 8 7 6 5 4 3 2 1

Library of Congress Cataloging-in-Publication Data

Rodgers, Alan, 1958-
   Temperature / Alan Rodgers and Angella Streluk.
      p. cm. -- (Measuring the weather)
Summary: Provides an introduction to temperature, examining how it is
measured and the relationship between temperature and weather.
Includes bibliographical references and index.
   ISBN 1-58810-689-6 -- ISBN 1-40340-129-2 (pbk.)
   1. Atmospheric temperature--Juvenile literature. [1. Atmospheric
temperature. 2. Weather.] I. Streluk, Angella, 1961- II. Title.
   QC901.A1 R64 2002
   551.5′25--dc21
                                   2002004027

Acknowledgments
The author and publishers are grateful to the following for permission to reproduce copyright
material: A. McLure (The Met Office): p. 4; Trevor Clifford Photography: pp. 6, 7, 8, 10, 13, 23, 25;
Science Photo Library: pp. 9, 14, 20; Robert Harding Picture Library: p. 12; Eye Ubiquitous: p. 16;
The Met Office/Crown: p. 18; Geoscience Features: p. 19; Bruce Coleman Collection: p. 27.

Cover photograph reproduced with permission of Tudor Photography and Photodisc.

Every effort has been made to contact copyright holders of any material reproduced in this
book. Any omissions will be rectified in subsequent printings if notice is given to the publisher.

Some words are shown in bold, **like this.** You can find out
what they mean by looking in the glossary.

Contents

Temperature and the Weather

We all feel the effects of hot and cold temperatures, but are we aware of the effect that the temperature has on the weather in general? How can we tell exactly how hot or cold it is? There is a lot to learn about measuring the temperature.

The weather reports that we see on the television and in newspapers come from professional **meteorologists.** They carefully take measurements of the weather from all around the world. Meteorologists all take measurements in the same way, so that they can share **data.** This helps meteorologists build up a picture of the weather around the world. This data is also very useful for local weather forecasters. A good knowledge of how the weather usually behaves in one area can help weather forecasters predict what it will be like each day. The changes in temperature are part of a day's experience of weather. In some places, the weather is similar every day, all year round. In other places, the weather is different for each season. **Climate** is the word used to describe the way the weather behaves over a long period of time.

Taking the various temperature readings that are needed to predict and record the weather helps us build up a picture of the weather. All professional meteorologists, like the man on the right, take these readings in the same way. This is so they can share and compare their data.

Temperature influences the type of weather in a place. The sun is the driving power behind the weather. Because warm air rises and cool air sinks, the heat of the sun stirs up the air in the **atmosphere.** This constant movement of air affects **air pressure,** wind, rain, and snowfall. For example, the wind is caused by air being sucked in to replace rising warm air. Different parts of the world are heated up differently for lots of reasons.

Temperature influences the way we dress, the things we do, and, sometimes, the safety of living things. There are many reasons why businesses need to know the temperature and the predicted temperature. For example, they need to consider how well people work in different temperatures.

Be careful!

Do not look directly at the Sun when studying the weather. Also, never take shelter under trees during a thunderstorm, because they could be hit by lightning.

These are some of the international symbols used by weather reporters. Weather reporters try to use the same symbols so that they can understand each other's charts.

The symbols on the left are used to show how much of the sky is covered by clouds. The signs on the right are used to show what type of **precipitation** is present.

Weather Symbols

■ Cloud Cover		■ General	
◯	no clouds	🖊	drizzle
		•	rain
◑	⅛ or less	••	more rain
		✻	snow
◔	⅜	✻ ✻	more snow
◖	⅜	▽	showers
◑	⅘	↳	thunderstorm
◑	⅝	△	hail
◕	⅝	∞	haze
◑	⅞	≡	fog
●	overcast	⌒	rainbow
⊗	sky obscured	⌒	dew

5

The Thermometer

Temperature is measured with a **thermometer.** A basic thermometer has a thin glass tube with no air in it. At the bottom of this tube is a **bulb** filled with liquid that expands and contracts as the temperature changes. The liquid takes up more room as the temperature gets higher and less room as the temperature drops. In most thermometers the liquid used is colored alcohol. Professional **meteorologists** use mercury instead of alcohol because it is more accurate. Mercury is an unusual metal, because it is normally in liquid—and not solid—form.

The glass tube is mounted on a **calibrated** scale, which means that readings can be compared. There are two main scales used for measuring temperatures, called **Celsius** and **Fahrenheit.**

There are several special types of thermometer. Some are made to be placed in the ground, on the ground, or in the air. Others have special features, like ways of recording the highest and lowest temperatures over a period of time.

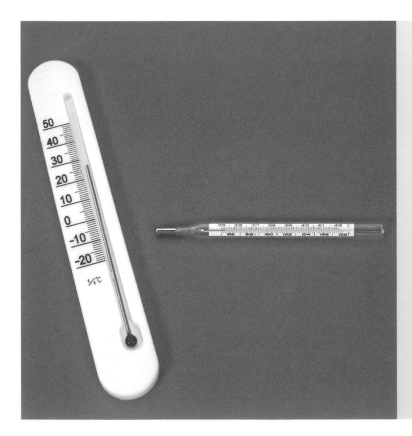

The red liquid in the thermometer on the left is colored alcohol. This thermometer is used for measuring normal temperatures (in your house, for example). The readings on this particular thermometer are in Celsius. although they could also be in Fahrenheit. The thermometer with the silver liquid is a mercury thermometer, used for special purposes. This one is for taking a person's temperature.

Digital thermometers

Digital thermometers can be very useful and are quite cheap to buy. Some record the highest and lowest temperatures. Others just display the current temperature. The **sensor** can be placed where you want to know the temperature, such as outside in the shade. The display unit can then be kept indoors, where it can be easily read.

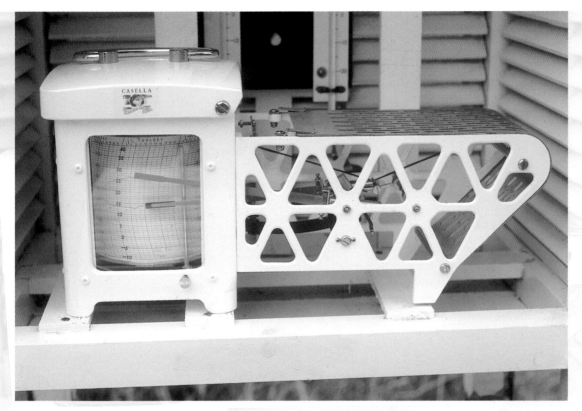

This **thermohygrograph** measures the temperature and humidity (see page 22) continuously. It records the **data** on a slowly revolving chart. A special metal strip reacts to the changes in temperature. These types of instruments are often used to record temperature in museums where it is important to make sure that valuable items do not get too hot or too cold.

Be safe!
- Thermometers are delicate instruments and should be handled carefully.
- Use alcohol thermometers, as mercury is very poisonous to touch if the thermometer breaks.
- Only use a thermometer for measuring temperature.

Reading the Temperature

It is important that all **meteorologists** follow the same rules for reading the temperature, so that their **data** can be compared. The **thermometer** is always put at a height of 4 feet (1.22 meters) above the ground. Temperature readings always need to be taken in the shade. Professional meteorologists keep their thermometers in a special box called a Stevenson Screen. This box keeps the thermometer out of the sun. The thermometer can also be put on a fence in the shade. The thermometer should face north in the northern **hemisphere** and south in the southern hemisphere, so that the Sun cannot fall directly on the liquid in the thermometers. A temperature taken in this way is called the **dry bulb temperature.** It can help to work out how much moisture is in the air.

Before reading a thermometer, check that there are no breaks in the column of liquid. This would give an inaccurate reading. To get an accurate reading, your eyes need to be level with the top of the liquid. If you look at the thermometer from above or below, your reading will be wrong.

These three pictures were taken when the thermometer was at the same temperature. Why do they all give different readings? Which one was taken from above, which from below, and which from a point level with the observer's eyes? You can find the answers on page 31.

Thermometers have a scale that is used to figure out the readings. Not all of the numbers on the scale can be put on the thermometer, so you have to figure out what each line on the scale represents. Work quickly when you take a reading. Your own body temperature, and breathing on the thermometer, can affect the accuracy of the reading. After you have made a reading, ask yourself if that reading makes sense.

Using temperature data

Many people need accurate temperature readings. For example, people who make and sell food need to be sure their products are kept at the right temperatures. The colder it is outside, the easier it is to keep food products cold, and the less money they have to spend on refrigeration.

When extra electricity is needed suddenly, because of hot or cold weather, power stations need to be able to produce it quickly. Here, in the control center, engineers figure out how much electricity is needed. Monitoring the weather forecast will help them to predict how much electricity people will need.

Maximum and Minimum Temperatures

A maximum and minimum **thermometer** can record the highest and lowest temperatures over a period of time. The temperature rises and falls several times during the day. If the temperature is only read once a day, these changes will be missed. Using maximum and minimum thermometers may show that a warm **front,** with its warm air, has passed between readings. The minimum temperature at night is often just before dawn. This low reading would be missed if the temperature was only read at the usual time of nine A.M.

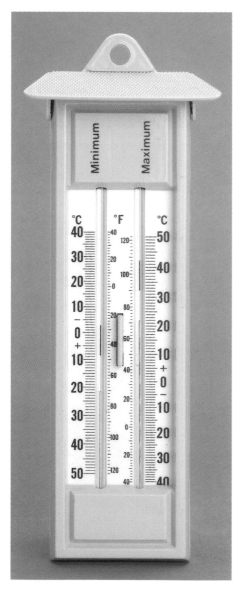

Six's thermometer

A Six's thermometer has one U-shaped tube. Liquid is used to push a small amount of mercury around the tube. The mercury forces small pins upward. These pins stay in that "up" position when the mercury falls, marking the highest point that the liquid has reached. Its markings are not like those of an ordinary thermometer. On one side, the numbers are higher at the top and lower at the bottom. On the other side, the scale is reversed (upside down). Readings are taken from the bottom of the pins that are pushed up by the mercury.

James Six was a dedicated **meteorologist.** He grew tired of getting up in the night to read the temperature! So, he invented this form of maximum and minimum thermometer.

Once the readings have been checked, the pins are pushed down again to sit on the top of the measuring liquid by pressing a button, or by placing a small magnet alongside the tube. The magnet attracts the metal pins down. When the thermometers have been reset, they should give readings that agree with the **dry bulb temperature.**

Try this with a friend!

Try reading the temperature very accurately every hour during the day to see when the maximum and minimum temperatures occurred.

- Read the temperature every hour.
- Draw a graph of the temperatures.
- Mark the maximum and minimum temperatures.
- Repeat on a different day and compare the results.

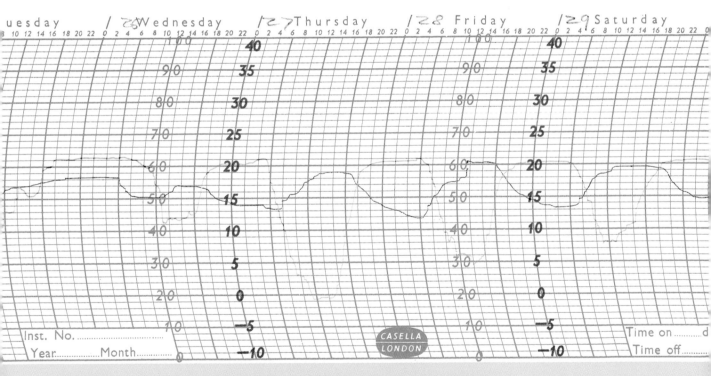

The **data** on this graph shows the extremes of temperature, which would be missed if you just recorded the dry bulb temperature once a day. The **thermohygrograph** has recorded the data constantly. The pen marking the temperature rises and falls as the temperature does. The maximum and minimum temperatures are shown by the black line on this chart.

Hot and Cold

Depending on the amount of sunlight we get, the temperature of the air around us can be higher or lower. The amount of sunlight can vary if objects like clouds get in the way. It can also vary depending on where in the world you are. Places nearer to the **equator** receive the most direct and strongest rays of the Sun. The further away from the equator you get, the weaker the rays will be.

You can record the rise and fall in temperature during the day. However, the temperature recorded on one particular day cannot tell you about the **climate** in a region. To give you this information, **data** recorded over a long period (several years) is needed. Then the data from a region can be looked at to see what the weather for each season is usually like.

Adapting to extreme temperatures

In a cold climate, people wear more clothes to keep them warm. In a hot climate, wearing white clothing reflects the heat away from your body. Architecture can tell you a lot about a region's climate. Even before air conditioning, there were ways of keeping cool. In hot countries, some buildings have tall wind towers with special **vents,** which help move air into living areas. Roofs can be built to adapt to the weather. For example, in wet countries steep roofs are built so that the rainwater can run off them.

This house in Queensland, Australia, is built on stilts so that air will move around and cool the house down. This is very useful in a hot climate.

Try this with a friend!

The terms "hot" and "cold" depend upon the temperature people are used to. A person used to Alaskan winters would consider a cold day in Melbourne, Australia to be very warm! Try this activity to show how the terms *hot* and *cold* can be misleading.

- Set up three bowls of water, each with a different temperature. Make one cold (50°F [10°C]), one medium (77°F [25°C]), and one hot (95°F [35°C]).
- Ask a friend to place their hand in the bowl of cold water for a short while.
- Ask your friend to then move their hand to the bowl of medium-temperature water.
- Ask them what they think the temperature feels like. Repeat the process, starting with the hot water this time.

Soil Temperature

Farmers and gardeners need to know the best time to plant their seeds. They do not want to waste money by sowing seeds when they will not grow. They know the best **germination** temperature for their plants, and they check this by using a soil **thermometer.** A soil thermometer tells them the temperature just below the surface of the soil. For example, peas germinate at a minimum temperature of 39° F (4° C). The farmer will wait until the soil has been this temperature for a few days before he plants his pea seeds.

The temperature of the soil is very different from the temperature of the air. Air temperature rises and falls quite quickly because the molecules in the air are spread out and can move about easily. This means that they can move heat around more quickly. The soil temperature changes more slowly because the soil takes longer to warm up or cool down. The deeper the soil, the slower the temperature will be to change. Longer thermometers are used to read the temperature deeper under the surface. Gardeners usually use a thermometer inside a metal tube. This tube can be put in the soil so that the soil thermometer can be easily removed and read.

This farmer knows that the seeds he is planting have a good chance of growing. He has checked to see that the average soil temperature is warm enough for germination.

Deep in the soil

A deep soil thermometer shows very gradual changes in temperature.
It usually shows the change in soil temperature over the seasons.
A shallow soil reading will show changes in temperature during the day.

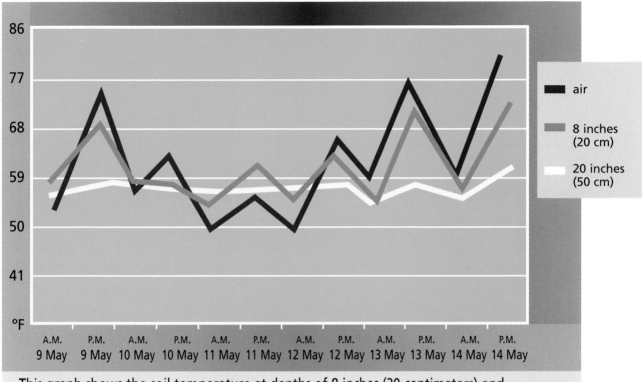

■	air	
■	8 inches (20 cm)	
■	20 inches (50 cm)	

This graph shows the soil temperature at depths of 8 inches (20 centimeters) and 20 inches (50 centimeters). It also shows the air temperature. Notice how the air temperature changes the most. Have you noticed that the temperature of the soil is different at depths of 8 inches (20 centimeters) and 20 inches (50 centimeters)?

Be accurate!

- Read a soil thermometer quickly before it starts to show the air temperature!
- Do not hold the thermometer by its **bulb** or you will take your own temperature.
- Keep the thermometer out of direct sunlight when you read it (turn your back to the Sun).
- Hold the top of the liquid level with your eyes to read it.
- If water gets into your thermometer tube in the ground, use some cloth on a stick to soak it up.

Grass Temperature and Frost

Meteorologists place their **thermometers** 4 feet (1.22 meters) above the ground. However, the difference between this temperature and the temperature at ground level can be large. Many people need to know the ground or grass temperature. For example, if it gets very cold, people in charge of keeping the roads clear of ice and snow send out trucks to put salt on them. They use **digital** thermometers linked to an alarm, which goes off when it gets cold enough for the roads to need salt.

Professional weather watchers use a special grass minimum thermometer. If a grass minimum thermometer is used, it needs to be set just above the level of short grass. It needs to be placed so that the **bulb** end is 1 to 2 inches (2.5 to 5 centimeters) above the ground, but just touching the top of the grass. Surface temperatures are always measured on grass so that **data** can be compared. If the ground temperature were measured on different surfaces, readings could not be compared. However, if there is no grass, the local soil may be used.

Sending out vehicles to spread salt onto ice is expensive. Accurate data reveals when salting is necessary. Lives may depend on these decisions.

Frost

Sometimes objects near the ground cool very quickly. This causes the moisture in the air to **condense**, forming tiny droplets of water called dew. When the ground cools below freezing—32°F (0°C)—the moisture turns directly into the powdery white crystals known as frost. Frost can damage delicate plants and weaken concrete that is setting.

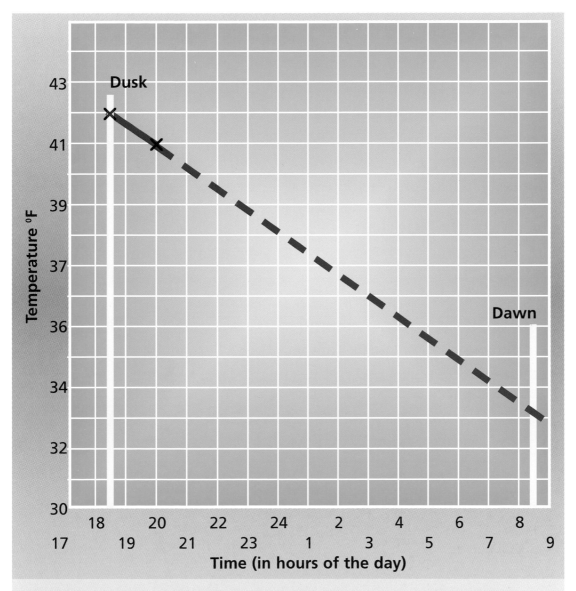

It is possible to forecast frost on a clear night if you know the times of dusk and dawn. Take the temperature just after sunset and then again about 90 minutes later. By this time the temperature should continue to fall at the same rate, unless the sky clouds over (this would make it warmer). Plot the temperatures on the graph and draw a straight line through them. Continue the line along the same path (this is called extrapolating). If the line goes below zero before dawn, there will be a frost.

Sensing Temperature with a Computer

Maximum and minimum **thermometers** record the highest and lowest temperatures during a period of time. In between these times the temperature can go up and down and not be recorded by that type of thermometer. By using electronic devices like computers, the temperature can be constantly monitored and recorded. This helps us understand the relationship between temperature and other factors in the weather. It has the advantage of monitoring the weather without someone having to be present all of the time. This is helpful in places such as schools, because **data** can be recorded during breaks. Computers can also be used to record weather in places that are difficult to live in, such as the Arctic or the tops of mountains.

Sharing information

Many **meteorologists** have access to a **weather station** linked to a computer. This is an accurate and easy way to collect weather data. This data can be put into computer programs, such as spreadsheets and databases. The data can then be used to make graphs to help predict what the weather will be like in the future. Files can be sent as attachments via e-mail and placed directly onto websites.

Data is collected by weather stations even in the middle of oceans, giving warnings about forthcoming weather. This means that bad weather (storms for example) can be predicted. Weather stations like this are especially important as oceans cover 70 percent of the world!

Collecting data

Web cams—cameras used to make video recordings and broadcast them over the Internet—can be used to view conditions around the world. You can find out a lot by looking at these pictures. For example, the clothes people are wearing can tell you about the weather in that place.

Temperature **sensors** can be used on their own or with other devices like computers. The greenhouses used to grow food and flowers need to have carefully controlled temperatures. Sensors read the temperature inside. They are linked to control units which are used to open and shut windows. If the temperature gets too high, the windows are opened. This cools the greenhouse down. Sensors can also control the heating and cooling systems of buildings. Buildings can have sensors that monitor temperatures and turn on the heating when there is a danger of the pipes freezing. Modern vehicles can be automatically heated or cooled depending on the outside weather conditions.

Automatic weather stations, like this one, monitor many weather features, including maximum and minimum temperature, current temperature, **air pressure,** wind strength and direction, and humidity. They also record sunshine and windchill.

Temperature through the Atmosphere

There is often a noticeable difference between the readings of a grass **thermometer** on the ground and the air around you—so imagine how different the temperature might be high up in the sky. The weather we experience only occurs in the lowest part of the **atmosphere.** Weather balloons are used to collect information about the weather in the highest points of this part of the atmosphere.

Temperature in the atmosphere is influenced by **air pressure.** The air around you has weight that presses down on everything. Although you can't feel it, the air pressure at sea level is about three times greater than at the top of Mount Everest.

Weather balloons measure the temperature and a lot of other weather **data.** They are used to build up a picture of the weather at different heights. This creates a worldwide picture of the weather. About one thousand **weather stations** around the world release these balloons.

Layers in the atmosphere

The atmosphere is divided into several levels that do not mix very well. The temperature at these levels varies, rising and falling, as you can see on the diagram below. The troposphere is between six and ten miles (ten and sixteen kilometers) thick. All of the clouds are made in this layer, and they produce hail, rain, snow, thunder, and lightning. These all affect the temperature. In the troposphere, the temperature falls the higher up you go. Airplanes try to fly above the weather in the troposphere. They fly up into the next layer of the atmosphere, the stratosphere, to make it more comfortable for passengers. Crossing from the troposphere to the stratosphere can be bumpy, but once there the journey is usually smoother.

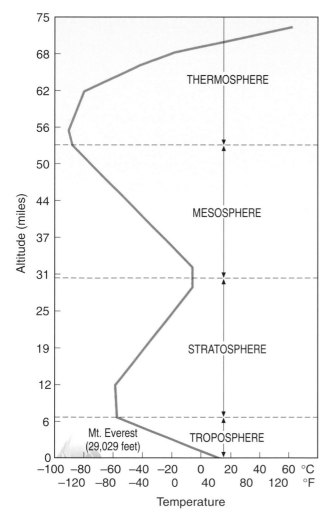

In the stratosphere, a gas called ozone absorbs energy from the Sun. This makes the temperature rise. Although the temperature rises, it is still very cold. Above this level is the mesosphere, where the air is at low pressure and the temperature falls again. The final layer, the thermosphere, is also known as the "hot layer." The Sun's rays warm this part of the atmosphere. Although the thermosphere goes up to about 311 miles (500 kilometers), it is very hot (3,632° F [2000° C]). Beyond the thermosphere is the **exosphere.**

The layers of the atmosphere do not go from one extreme of temperature to the other. Each layer has its own special conditions.

Humidity

Moisture is constantly escaping from rivers, lakes, the ground, and plants. Because of this, all air contains water vapor. The amount of water vapor in the air is measured as humidity on a scale from zero to one hundred and is given as a percentage. This percentage is known as relative humidity. When the relative humidity is 100 percent, the air is full of water and the water vapor becomes fog.

Dew

Dew is water vapor that has **condensed** as the air gets cooler. It forms when the air temperature has reached **dew point.** Even in a desert, the air is not completely dry and the water vapor in it forms dew in the evening. At night, the air cools quickly as the ground gives off the heat it has collected during the day. The water then condenses out of the air. Some plants in dry **climates** arrange their leaves so that they can collect this dew. This makes up for the lack of rain and means that they can survive.

The Heat Index

Our comfort is affected by the relative humidity, especially when combined with high temperatures. When the humidity is high, the temperature feels hotter than it really is. The Heat Index (HI) is used to explain this condition. People who take part in energetic sports are aware that the Heat Index can affect their performance. When choosing places to hold sports events, the organizers must consider an area's relative humidity.

How humidity makes us feel hotter			
Dry conditions (Little moisture in the air)	Very warm	Hot	Very hot
Humid conditions (Lots of moisture in the air)	Feels hot	Feels very hot	Feels extremely hot

This table shows how temperature and humidity affect how comfortable we feel. The Heat Index also affects how likely you are to get **heat stroke.**

Try this yourself!

It is possible to make a **hygrometer** to measure humidity.
Use soft paper that can absorb moisture easily.

- Make a balance with a drinking straw threaded onto some paper clip wire. Rest it on a cardboard pivot.
- Thread squares of dry paper onto one end of the straw.
- Draw a scale at the other end using the other end of the straw as a pointer.
- An increase in humidity will make the paper end heavier and make the pointer at the other end move up.

Wet and Dry Bulb Temperatures

You can find out the relative humidity by using a pair of special **thermometers** called a wet and dry bulb **hygrometer.** One thermometer has its **bulb** wrapped in a wet **wick.** The other thermometer is left exposed to the air. When water changes from a liquid into water vapor, it uses up energy. The energy it uses is heat. The temperature of the thermometer with its bulb wrapped in the wet wick goes down, because the water in the wick evaporates.

The difference between the temperatures of the pair of wet and dry bulb thermometers is used to work out the relative humidity. If it is a warm, dry day there will be a big difference between the wet and dry thermometers. This means the relative humidity will be low. If it is a damp day, there will be less difference. This means the relative humidity will be high.

Finding the relative humidity

The table below shows part of a relative humidity chart. To find the humidity, read the dry and then the wet bulb temperatures. Next, locate the **dry bulb temperature** on the top of the chart. Then find the wet bulb temperature on the left side of the chart. Read down and across from these numbers to find the relative humidity. For example, if the dry bulb temperature is 63°F (i), and the wet bulb temperature is 56°F (ii), the relative humidity is 64 percent (iii).

Humidity Chart						
Dry bulb Temperature / Wet bulb Temperature	61° F	62° F	(i)63° F	64° F	65° F	66° F
55° F	68%	64%	60%	56%	52%	48%
(ii)56° F	73%	69%	(iii)64%	60%	56%	53%
57° F	78%	74%	69%	65%	61%	57%
58° F	84%	79%	74%	70%	66%	61%

Remember that humidity readings should fit in with the type of weather you are experiencing. This will depend on your location. Very low readings, such as ten percent, are usually only found in deserts.

Other hygrometers

There are other sorts of hygrometers. For example, a whirling hygrometer is a portable hygrometer for use away from a **weather station.** It has its own pair of matching thermometers. One of them is connected, by a wick, to a container of water. Using a **weather house hygrometer** is another way of finding out how humid it is. A special kind of material inside the model house changes length when it is humid. When that happens, a small male figure comes out with his umbrella (see below). This is supposed to predict rain.

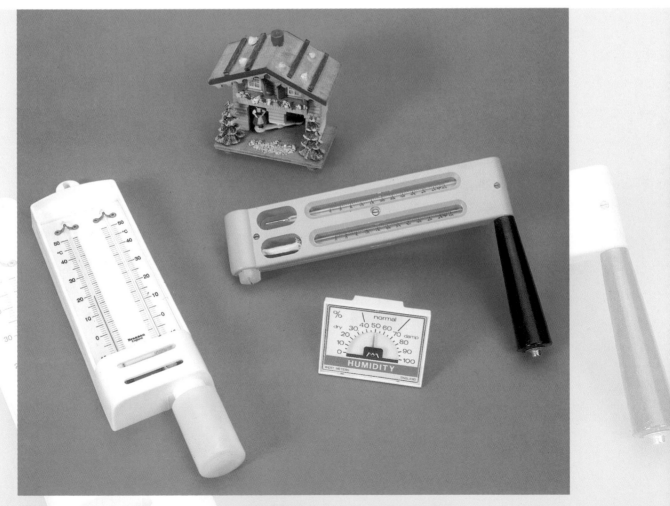

Can you tell which hygrometer is which? Use the text above to help you. One of the hygrometers above (which is not mentioned in the text) is a dial hygrometer. It uses human hair, which changes length depending upon humidity levels.

Cold Fronts and Warm Fronts

When you look at a weather map of a large area, you can see very large air masses. Air masses are made up of air that contains the same amount of moisture and that is of a similar temperature. High up, the **atmosphere** is made up of lots of these air masses. They start from two main places on the Earth—the very hot **tropical** regions and the very cold polar regions. They are always moving. If they travel over a lot of sea, they pick up moisture and are called maritime air masses. They are called continental air masses if they travel over a lot of dry land (and become drier). These air masses bring us different types of weather, depending on where the air came from and what it traveled over.

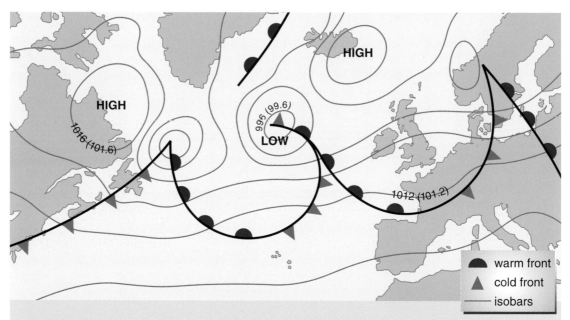

Knowing the type of air mass and how it is moving will help predict the weather. This type of map shows this information. Cold **fronts** are shown by blue triangles. Red semicircles show warm fronts. The numbers show the air pressure in millibars (kiloPascals are in parentheses), which are units that measure air pressure.

Origination of the four main air masses, and the weather they bring		
	Starting from polar regions (very cold)	**Starting from tropical regions (very hot)**
Traveled over land (continental)	Cold and dry	Hot and dry
Traveled over sea (maritime)	Cold and wet	Hot and wet

Weather maps

The main thing you will notice about a real weather map or chart is that it is covered in dark, circular lines called isobars. These lines link together areas of equal **air pressure.** When you see lots of lines close together, you are looking at a very windy area.

When one air mass stays still over us, our weather will stay the same. If one air mass is replaced by another, the weather will change. The boundary between these two air masses is called a front. Where there are fronts, the weather is unsettled and often stormy.

A warm front is the edge of a warm air mass that is approaching a cold air mass. When the warm air mass slides over the cold air mass, various clouds appear, finishing with clouds that bring **precipitation.** A cold front is the edge of a cold air mass. It has a steep bulging edge, which produces **heaped** clouds, and can bring heavy rain as it pushes underneath a warm air mass. It gets very windy as the cold front gets nearer. A cold front also brings different clouds, sometimes ending with **cumulonimbus.**

Air near the **equator** is hotter than air in other areas of the world. Hot air is less **dense** and rises. Cold air is denser and sinks. This starts off the movement of air in the atmosphere. The swirling clouds in this picture show this movement of air.

Temperature and the Environment

The difference in the amount of sunshine in different places means that there are differences in temperature around the world. Overall, the temperature near the **equator** is much hotter and the area in the polar regions is much colder. Most plants and animals live in the **temperate** and **tropical** areas. Life is easier in these areas. The **climate** of colder regions makes it a struggle to survive there.

The greenhouse effect

Lots of people are worried about the rise in temperature on the Earth. This has been named the greenhouse effect. Certain gases in the **atmosphere** help to keep some of the heat that comes off the Earth from disappearing into space. There is a balance, however, between keeping in enough heat to keep us warm and keeping in too much heat. Some gases prevent too much heat from leaving our atmosphere. These are often called greenhouse gases.

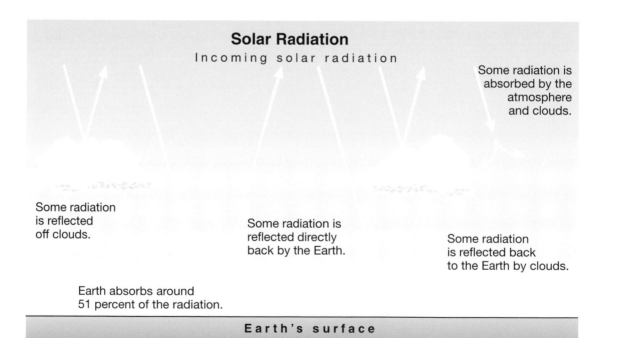

Solar Radiation

Incoming solar radiation

Some radiation is absorbed by the atmosphere and clouds.

Some radiation is reflected off clouds.

Some radiation is reflected directly back by the Earth.

Some radiation is reflected back to the Earth by clouds.

Earth absorbs around 51 percent of the radiation.

Earth's surface

Heat from the Sun warms the Earth. This heat comes from solar radiation. When this heat is reflected back by the Earth, some of it is prevented from leaving the atmosphere by greenhouse gases. The difference between the heat kept and lost affects the temperature of the Earth.

Rising water levels

Some human activities may be dangerously increasing these gases. This could result in a rise in temperature worldwide, which would melt the ice at the poles. Sea levels would rise and areas of low-lying land would disappear under the water. This would leave less space to live in and less land for growing crops. Communities built near the sea would disappear, along with the services they provided for the rest of the world. Most of the goods in the world are transported in ships, which need harbors where these goods can be loaded and unloaded. Many harbors would disappear under the water if the oceans rose.

Meteorologists are studying the way these gases are changing our weather and climate. Measuring the weather can help us understand the world we live in and help plan the way we will live in the future.

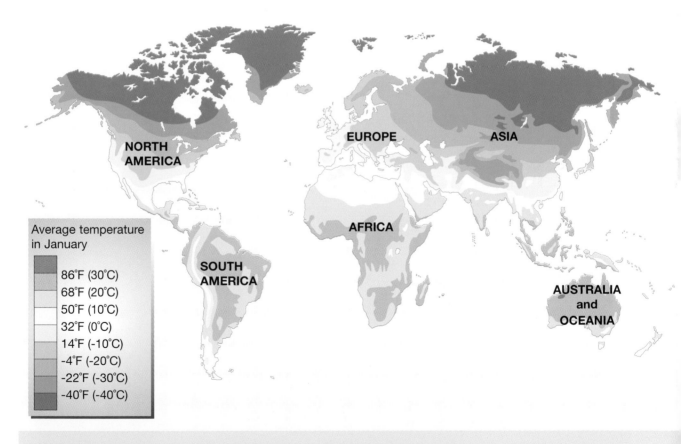

Average temperature in January

	86°F (30°C)
	68°F (20°C)
	50°F (10°C)
	32°F (0°C)
	14°F (-10°C)
	-4°F (-20°C)
	-22°F (-30°C)
	-40°F (-40°C)

The colors on this map show worldwide temperatures in January. The colder weather is occurring in the northern **hemisphere.** It is summer in the southern hemisphere. These temperatures may be changing slowly.

Glossary

air pressure pressure, at the surface of the Earth, caused by the weight of the air in the atmosphere

atmosphere gases that surround the planet

bulb rounded end of the glass tube of a thermometer, containing the measuring liquid

calibrated describes an instrument that is accurately set and marked to read particular measurements

Celsius scale used in thermometers like those constructed by Anders Celsius (1701–44). In this scale, the freezing point of water is 0° and the boiling point is 100°.

climate general weather conditions of an area over a long period of time

condense turn from a gas into a liquid

cumulonimbus dark, heaped cloud of great height, which often brings showers and thunderstorms

data set of facts that can be investigated to get information

dense thick, closely packed

dew point temperature at which a vapor begins to condense

digital shown as numbers or turned into data that can be understood by a computer

dry bulb temperature temperature taken from a thermometer exposed to the air

equator imaginary horizontal line around the center of the Earth, at equal distance from both the north and south poles

exosphere highest layer of Earth's atmosphere, the one next to space

Fahrenheit temperature scale invented in 1714 by Gabriel Daniel Fahrenheit. In this scale, the freezing point of water is 32° and the boiling point is 212°.

front front edge of an air mass, where the air mass meets air of a different temperature

germination the first stages of growth in a seed

heaped piled up in mounds

heat stroke illness caused by the body overheating and becoming dehydrated (not having enough water). It is common when it is very hot and humid outside.

hemisphere half of the globe, usually the northern or southern half

hygrometer instrument for measuring humidity or water vapor content

meteorologist person who collects weather data and studies the weather

precipitation moisture that falls from clouds in a variety of forms, including rain, snow, and hail

sensor instrument for measuring a physical change, such as temperature

temperate areas that are neither too hot nor too cold

thermohygrograph instrument for recording humidity and temperature on a chart

thermometer instrument for measuring temperature

tropical very warm and wet

vent opening that lets air in or out

weather house hygrometer toy house with two tiny figures inside, a woman and a man. When the woman comes out, it will be dry. When the man comes out, it will rain.

weather station set of weather-measuring instruments placed in an appropriate location

wick specially woven piece of cloth that can pull liquid up into it

More Books to Read

Gardner, Robert and Eric Kemer. *Science Projects about Temperature and Heat.* Berkeley Heights, N.J.: Enslow Publishers, 1994.

Morgan, Sally. *Changing Climate.* Danbury, Conn.: Franklin Watts, 1999.

Walpole, Brenda. *Temperature.* Milwaukee, Wisc.: Gareth Stevens Incorporated, 1995.

Answer to question on page 8: The thermometer on the left was viewed level, the thermometer in the middle from below, and the thermometer at right from above.

Index